FOOTBALL
FOR BEGINNERS

Everything You Need to Know to Enjoy a Match from Scratch in Less than 1 Hour | Game Techniques and Strategies for Tomorrow's Champions Included

Winthrop Chavez

Table of Contents

INTRODUCTION

Football is a hugely popular sport in the United States, but many people really don't understand how it works. Even if you're not interested in playing football yourself, you may have watched your favorite player score an incredible touchdown and wanted to celebrate with some knowledge of your own.

Whether you go to NFL games, watch them on TV, listen to talk radio or read articles online – this is the book for you. I've written Football for Beginners with all of you in mind, so whether you are a male or female, mother or father, beginner or veteran – there's always something new to learn and enjoy.

This book will teach you about the game of football and how to watch it like a pro. You will learn the basics of offense, defense, special teams, and more. Watching matches will never be quite the same once you're armed with this knowledge.

You'll get to know the history of the sport, not just in the US, but worldwide – and perhaps most importantly, you will learn who invented it. Perhaps it's time to give thanks to those who came before us!

Of course, one of this book's major focuses is on football in America, a sport that has been around for over three hundred years. For this reason, there is a lot of information about the game's history.

Chapter 1

HISTORY AND ORIGINS OF AMERICAN FOOTBALL

What Is American Football?

The solution might be the first lesson we learn on this journey. You may be wondering why I made care to put "American" before football. First of all, excellent question! Second, I did this for two reasons. First off, soccer is our version of "football," as it is known in other areas of the world, specifically in Europe. That's right, if you go to Germany and start shouting "football this" and "football that," the wonderful people there will probably assume you're talking about soccer. To be clear, there are two more well-known football leagues around the world: the Canadian Football League (CFL) and the Australian Football League (AFL). These two leagues have significantly different regulations than our league, the National Football League (NFL), and that may make for interesting reading for a second or third book. It's important to keep in mind that this book solely discusses the NFL!

Let's go on to the topic of this chapter now that that has been addressed. Unfortunately, you have to learn a bit about the fundamentals before you can dive right into the fun. We shall discover a little bit about the history and evolution of football in this chapter. This modification largely concentrates on items like league changes, uniforms, and player safety.

In order to better understand some terminologies and words as we continue to deepen our understanding of this fantastic game, it is crucial to study the fundamentals of the sport!

How and when was football invented?

The question of "Who came up with all of this stuff?" arises when you consider all the strange rules, laws, and concepts that go into a typical football game. We need to go back to November 12, 1892, which was over 120 years ago, for this. The Pittsburgh Athletic Club football team lost against the Allegheny Athletic Association on this particular day. Even though none of this was very significant because football had already been played before, William "Pudge" Heffelfinger was the first to get payment for participating in the game on this occasion. He received $500, which is equivalent to little more than $15,000 in today's money. Mr. Pudge, that's not terrible for one game!

Few people were surprised to learn that football was created by combining rugby and soccer, two popular sports at the time. Rutgers and Princeton squared off in the first-ever football game in 1869. However, it wasn't until the 1880s that rule modifications began to transform a completely untamed game into the football that we know and love today. Walter Camp, a Yale rugby player, was the person behind the amendments to the rules.

Most athletic clubs established football teams by the 1880s (ProFootballHallofFame, n.d.). It should come as no surprise that collegiate athletes loved the competitive part of football, as games frequently ended in brawls. It was a method for college students to let their aggression out after a long day of classes because it was a contact sport.

All of this was to prepare the arena for the infamous match between the Pittsburgh Athletic Club and the Allegheny Athletic Association (AAA vs. PAC). In what was soon turning into a bitter rivalry, both clubs were striving for a competitive edge. However, it was the PAC who eventually paid Pudge to join their team, making Pudge the first-ever professional athlete.

The two teams kept looking for superior players in the region after the game to improve their chances of defeating the opposition the next time an opportunity presented itself. The PAC visited Chicago for scouting purposes before flying back to Pennsylvania to face the AAA again. Pudge and Knowlton "Snakes" Ames of the Chicago squad were both paid by the PAC to represent the PAC in its forthcoming fight with the AAA.

However, the AAA did not consider the action to be casual. Thus informed, the AAA conducted some independent scouting and discovered that Ed Malley and star end Ben "Sport" Donnelly would play for the AAA. (n.d.). As a result, the PAC and AAA each had some "extra ammunition" for their next match.

Oddly enough, Pudge scored just once during the contest, giving the game a final score of 4-0. That's wonderful if you think that's a strange score! In 1892, touchdowns were only worth four points, as opposed to the six points they are now. Following a touchdown (crossing the ball into the opposing end zone), you are permitted to kick a one-point extra point (field goal) or "go for 2," which entails positioning yourself close to the opposing team's goal line and attempting to score once more for an additional two points. A crucial element regarding the two-point conversion: You do not receive the one point you would have received for a field goal if it is unsuccessful. There is a small risk/reward dynamic at play here!

Funny enough, the AAA made a net profit of $621 from the old game against the PAC, which is more than $16,000 in today's money! Even though the game itself was slow and low-scoring, it nevertheless demonstrated that football offered plenty of financial opportunities for both players and team owners.

Who Invented It?

The origins of American football are a little less obvious than those of basketball and baseball, both of which can be traced down to a single person. While some place its inception in the 1820s, others contend that the "Pioneer Period" of 1869–1875 saw the sport's official establishment.

The majority of historians and football enthusiasts concur that the Pioneer Period gave rise to the real beginnings of modern American football.

On November 6, 1869, Rutgers University and Princeton University played the first football game that is recorded in history. Two teams of 25 players each competed in the game at Rutgers Field in an effort to score by kicking the ball into the opponent's field goal. The ball could not be carried or thrown! That contest was won by Rutgers 6-4. Although by current standards the 42-39 games were not quite as thrilling, they were nonetheless thrilling for all the fans present. Despite this, the game was still physically demanding, bloody, and violent.

Through the "football craze" that this game ignited, more and more teams began to play the game across the nation. By 1873, football was being played in front of spectators at the majority of institutions across the nation.

This paved the way for Walter Camp, known as the "Father of American Football," to succeed (Wikipedia, n.d.). The idea to reduce the number of players on each side from 15 to 11 was initially put forth in 1880 by Camp, a player and pioneer in the development of game regulations. Although this proposition was initially turned down, it ultimately became law in the late 1880s. The number Walter Camp suggested 141 years ago (and counting) is still 11, today.

The rule that has withstood the test of time was another of Camp's most well-known changes. "...the line of scrimmage's establishment and the quarterback's snap from the center were likewise passed in 1880." Let me briefly explain those four phrases because they can certainly be confusing to those who are unfamiliar with the game.

Line of Scrimmage: A team's possession of the ball begins at this point. The ball is placed here after the kickoff so that the team can start their attempt to advance down the field and score. The location of the line of scrimmage for the next play changes every time a team completes a pass or advances (or retreats!) the football.

Snap: This is not a snap from Thanos, no! The quarterback receives the ball from the center during the snap. In most plays, it opens. Until the ball is snapped, no player from either team may cross the line of scrimmage.

Center: The offensive team member who snaps the ball to the quarterback is known as the center. Of the five linemen, he is the third from the middle. Protecting the quarterback is the responsibility of offensive linemen, who are regarded as some of the largest players in football.

Quarterback: Most certainly, a quarterback comes to mind when you think about football. All quarterbacks, including Joe Montana, Peyton Manning, Tom Brady, Aaron Rodgers, and Joe Namath! The player who gets the snap from the center and chooses what to do with it while defenders are charging at him is the quarterback. He has a few options, including sprinting up the field himself, passing the ball to one of his players, or giving it to the running back, who is supposed to do just that.

I hope this helped make the quote a bit clearer, but there is a lot more to learn about all of these topics in the future.

Looking back, our friend Walter Camp hadn't yet finished transforming the game. Although his first intention was to introduce the line of scrimmage regulations to enhance activity and make the game more entertaining, he immediately recognized that teams—Princeton in particular—were using their players' new skills to hang onto the ball for prolonged periods of time and draw the game out. In other words, his strategy failed! He then put into effect the down and distance rule in 1882, which mandated that teams advance at least five yards in three plays before turning the ball over to the opposing team. Four plays of at least 10 yards each are required by this regulation, which has evolved over time and is now applied to modern American football.

The ability to tackle a player below the waist, referees, scoring guidelines, and halves were some of the other rules imposed by Camp. Some variation of each of these guidelines is still in use in the game today.

Camp left the game of football in 1882 but continued to attend rule conferences until his passing in 1925. To this day, All-American teams are still chosen in his honor by the Walter Camp Football Foundation (n.d.).

Walter Camp was a great innovator for the game, and his numerous rule modifications helped pave the way for the modern football that we all know and love. One of the most significant individuals in football history, he is regarded as the real father of American football (despite only playing for a few years).

However, despite the fact that his rule modifications were revolutionary at the time, football would continue to develop through the years, leading to further revisions in those rules. We will examine how laws have changed since the 19th century in this part as well as how they are still evolving.

The Evolution of Football Over Time

Games alter and develop over time, much like humans do. Football rules are always changing to meet the demands of fans, safety officials, and players, even though some of the older rules made sense for the time.

A Competition Committee has been established by the NFL to adjust the rules and modernize the game as necessary.

Today, rule modifications are put into place rather rapidly to increase player safety, but this was not the case when the NFL was established in 1920.

When a rule needed to be altered back then, it could take years or even decades for the change to take effect. Today, laws can be modified annually!

The NFL's first-ever playoff game in 1932 led to one of the organization's earliest significant adjustments. The Chicago Bears and the Portsmouth Spartans were the teams competing. In that contest, Bronko Nagurski, a future Hall of Fame fullback for the Chicago Bears, faked a plunge, stepped back, leapt, and completed a lob pass to Red Grange for a crucial score in his team's 9-0 triumph (NFL, n.d.).

At that point in the game, the quarterback (or whoever held the ball) was not permitted to toss it farther than five yards behind the line of scrimmage. To put it another way, the ball carrier needed to be at least 5 yards from the line of scrimmage before throwing a pass. A player could now throw the ball from anyplace behind the line of scrimmage after the league altered its rule in 1933, in part as a result of the fury that Portsmouth displayed following this game. The stipulation is still in place today.

The NFL has maintained that its main goal in proposing rule modifications is to increase the game's enjoyment and entertainment value for its fans. Hugh "Shorty" Ray, an NFL Hall of Famer for his rule modifications, "...cracked the data and identified a direct association between scoring and better attendance" (n.d.). As a result, the league started enforcing rules that would increase the game's offensive entertainment value, which the fans welcomed.

For the next 30 years or so, teams started putting more emphasis on rushing the ball than passing the ball, which caused the league to cool down on the adjustments and enter a type of lull. As a result, there were fewer plays, shorter games, and many bored spectators.

In an effort to revive the thrill of the game, the NFL launched a package in 1974. Among these new rules were:

- Making kicks more difficult by moving the goalposts back 10 yards.

- All field goals that are missed from further than the 20-yard line should result in an immediate turnover, giving the other team the ball where the kick was blocked.

- Kickoffs were moved from the 40 to the 35-yard line, which led to an increase in high-contact plays.

- lowering fines for offensive plays.

All of these regulations, along with a few others, were put in place to increase the sport's excitement and high-intensity action.

The outcome? increased passing yards per game and a decrease in rushing yards per game The league has definitely focused on becoming a more pass-happy league, much to the joy of fans, even though running the football is still a crucial component of the sport that teams still play in today's game! A 5-yard sprint is significantly less thrilling than a 30-yard toss down the field.

Not all game rules, however, were created with increased entertainment in mind. Later on, the league imposed restrictions on the "chop block," an extremely risky play in which two offensive players run down the field and block the same defensive player, one high and one low, frequently resulting in knee injuries for the defensive players. The chop block is a 15-yard penalty in the contemporary NFL, meaning the team that committed the foul must advance 15 yards before its subsequent play!

No matter how you feel about the NFL as a league, it's impressive to see them experiment with and adopt new regulations, something that other leagues like the Major League Baseball (MLB), National Basketball Association (NBA), and National Hockey League (NHL) occasionally find difficult.

How and Why the Uniforms Have Changed

There wasn't much of a uniform to speak of when football first started in the late 19th century. Players had very little padding, no helmets, and shabby-looking clothes. The gear has changed as the sport has progressed. We are better able to identify concussions and other head problems thanks to contemporary technologies, and we can make highly complex helmets to protect the athletes.

The Helmet

A match between the Army and the Navy in 1893 marked the debut of the football helmet. Some players thought about including helmets in the mix as people began to notice how risky the game could be for possible head and neck injuries. But football teams all around the nation were not required to wear helmets until 1939.

In order to protect players who were concerned for their personal safety, the original football helmets were made of leather straps or mole skin fused together (Daughters, 2013). Later, the "ear flap/aviator models" took their place because these rudimentary designs didn't accomplish much to protect players from harm.

Robert Zuppke, the coach at Illinois, introduced the first plastic helmet in the 1930s and 1940s. Although the plastic helmet initially experienced certain challenges due to factors like price and demand, they eventually overcame these challenges and replaced the leather helmets of the past.

Following that, athletes and teams started to paint school logos on their helmets to display their school loyalty. These helmets typically had eye-catching colors and stylish mascots and emblems for added style points!

However, in addition to this use, the bright helmets may also make it simpler for the quarterback to identify his receivers as they move downfield. Receivers are athletes that sprint down the field to locate open spaces so they can catch a pass. The quarterback could more quickly distinguish between his team's colors and those of the opposition because to their vividly colored headgear.

Early in the 1970s, Riddell once more established the benchmark with the release of the HA series of helmets, which had vinyl pads within the helmet that could be filled with air to further absorb impact and provide a more personalized fit (2013).

Since then, Riddell has been the leading helmet provider and closely collaborates with scientists to guarantee players' safety and comfort in their helmets.

Having the helmets at least somewhat comfortable is a pleasant luxury to have, even though safety should always come first!

The Facemask

It is far more difficult to pinpoint the facemask's beginnings. It shouldn't be surprising that punches and jabs were thrown at faces during practically every game considering that football was originally played by youthful college students who were wanting to let off some steam. As a result, several players created nose guards or other devices with a medieval appearance to protect their faces.

Riddell didn't create a facemask especially for Cleveland Browns quarterback Otto Graham until 1953. It's safe to say that it wasn't the first facemask used in football, but pinpointing the exact first facemask is practically difficult!

Graham was unfortunate since a Lucite shield was used to make his facemask. Even while it made sense on paper, the Lucite had a nasty propensity of shattering on impact, which led to its eventual NFL prohibition.

This prompted Riddell to introduce the BT-5 helmet with a built-in single-bar facemask, which set off a chain reaction that eventually resulted in the double-bar, triple-bar, and various bespoke facemasks that are used in the NFL today.

Riddell collaborates closely with scientists to develop the best facemask designs for optimal player safety, much like it does for its helmets.

The Shoulder Pads

Oddly enough, in football, the notion of shielding the upper body predates that of protecting the head. L.P. Smock is credited with creating shoulder pads in 1877. At the time, Smock was a Princeton student. The original shoulder pads were stitched onto jerseys were consisted of leather and wool.

Shoulder pads did not catch up to the era's helmets until the 1960s and 1970s. The pads could be made leaner and tougher by switching from leather to plastic, increasing their durability.

The areas that the shoulder pads were used to cover changed as the materials did. The plastic padding, which was initially reserved only for the shoulders, gradually migrated down the body to cover the ribs and upper chest.

The most startling equipment modification in terms of appearance was perhaps the change in shoulder pads around the turn of the 20th century. Players' frontsides evolved from a simple means of shoulder protection into a useful cocoon.

In contrast to the bulky pads of the 1990s, the effective protection also allowed players to appear sleek and swift. Although it may not seem significant to you and I, players value stylish padding and appearance because they are always in the public glare.

More than just cosmetic changes have been made to the new pads, as they now have better ventilation, increased movement, increased comfort, and improved protection (2013).

The Pants

The pants haven't changed all that much since football's invention in the late 19th century, compared to the helmet and shoulder pads. The majority of players began donning padded football pants in the late 1880s, far earlier than the helmet and facemask entered the game.

The early football pants featured canvas and pads sewed into the pants themselves, similar to the shoulder pads. Following that, evolution continued to advance until ultimately hip pads were included as well.

The equipment has evolved to be lighter, more streamlined, and cooler for contemporary players, just like all of the other gear we have discussed so far.

The pants' focus is on synthetic materials like nylon and other materials that are both incredibly comfortable and nearly invisible.

The shoes are now referred to as cleats. It's amazing how well those early college football players could move thanks to the boots-like equipment they wore. The footwear was awkward, clumsy, and slow.

Strangely enough, unlike some of the other pieces of equipment we have seen thus far, the advancement of technology did not lead to improved shoes for the players. No, it was instead partly brought about by fans' desire for more competitive activity. Better athletic footwear would result in better traction and more spectacular football plays.

The fact that players had to account for various weather conditions was another consideration in this decision. For example, while the boots were effective on a sunny day, conditions would deteriorate as it started to rain or snow. These elements worked together to create the cleats.

Cleats first appeared when players added metal to their boots to improve their traction in cold conditions, taking cues from professional baseball and European soccer.

From there, designers completely abandoned the boot design in favor of the lower, sleeker, and more sophisticated cleats.

The Ball

Football cannot exist without, well, the football! Anyone who is familiar with rugby will not be surprised to learn how similar the rugby ball and American football are. The rugby ball has a similar shape to the soccer ball, but it's bigger and composed of different materials.

But it wasn't always like that. It was a terrible cross between a rugby ball and a soft basketball that was utilized in the first game between Rutgers and Princeton in 1869. The ball was really challenging to toss, kick, or even hold because it wouldn't maintain its shape!

The first leather football was made in 1887 by Spalding, which at the time was better renowned for producing baseballs than footballs. The football was far more resemblant of the sleek football we know today than the one used in the Rutgers vs. Princeton game, although still being uncomfortable and rough on both sides.

"Evolution and necessity, rather than a predetermined rule, caused the pointy ends of the football to become more apparent through time, and the body to become more streamlined" (2013). In other words, the ball evolved much like all other components of football.

Up until 1956, teams used a white football for night games to make it easier to see in the dark, which is an intriguing but lesser-known fact about the ball. Even though a brown football with white stripes subsequently took its place, this concept is also supported by the following intriguing fact: While college football retained its white stripes, the NFL finally did not. College football teams still utilize a brown ball with white stripes, although the NFL uses a ball that is all brown.

Chapter 2

BENEFITS OF PLAYING THE SPORT OF FOOTBALL AND CONTRAINDICATIONS

Sportsmen and women across America love playing football. It has been a popular sport for decades, and it is not hard to see why. The game is fun and can be frustratingly intense at the same time. In this chapter, we will focus on the benefits of playing football. We will also look at any possible contraindications to playing the sport, as well as some other important concepts.

What are some of the benefits of playing football? Sports can provide a wide range of benefits. There is a lot you could get out of playing football; however, when you look at what is considered to be one of its most important aspects, it becomes clear why so many people enjoy playing the sport so much.

Health Benefits

One of the reasons that football is a very popular sport is that it has a lot of health benefits.

These are the most common ones:

1. Healthier Heart

Although heart disease is the leading cause of death in the USA, there is good news: multiple studies have shown that regular exercise from sports participation can significantly improve heart health and lower the risk of dying from cardiovascular disease. Although football is a very intense sport, it can be a good way to beat heart disease and improve overall health.

2. Lowering Stress Levels and Boosting Immunity

With an increased heart rate, researchers have shown that there are also lowered levels of stress hormones as well as higher levels of antibodies that aid in fighting off illness. From lowering stress to an increase in confidence, football has been shown to positively impact the immune system and overall health.

3. Reduced Risk of Chronic Disease

Although research on the effects of football has been inconclusive, it seems that there are several effects that occur when playing the sport. These include a reduction in blood pressure levels and cholesterol and more so, reduced risks of heart disease, cancer, and premature death.

4. Diverse Social Connections

People from a variety of backgrounds, occupations, and ages make up sports clubs and teams, but they are all brought together by their passion for the sport. It's an excellent method to mingle and make new friends.

Also, if you ever need help with anything or have a question, there are always people to help you out. This can be very beneficial as we all need help from time to time and it's good to know that you are likely to find someone willing and able to help if you need it.

5. Reduced Risk of Diabetes

To reduce the incidence of prediabetes and type 2 diabetes, the American Diabetes Association advises a mix of aerobic exercise and strength training. One of the biggest health benefits of playing football is that it increases both muscular strength and endurance.

Football makes the heart more active, allowing more oxygen to be distributed throughout the body, which will improve the effectiveness of the muscles and aid in burning excess fat. It can also help to strengthen bones prevent osteoporosis and build muscle mass, which is a necessity for a healthy heart.

6. Psychological Benefits

In addition to physical attributes, football players develop several important mental ones as well.

Studies have shown that football players have a higher sense of satisfaction with their lives as well as increased self-confidence and life skills. The mental benefits of football are often overlooked and underappreciated, but they are still incredibly valuable, and it is important to understand how playing the sport can affect the mind.

7. Sleep Better

In addition to the physical benefits of football, playing the sport can have a tremendous effect on your sleep patterns.

It is possible that this may be part of the reason why so many people love playing football and see it as a time for escaping reality for the day. Exposure to lights and noise during the game may be one reason why some players report sleeping better after a big game.

It is important to note that while this is common, this ringing in one's ears will fade away if they do not play otherwise. If you want to get the most out of your football playing experience, you should not just play the game, but also stay active in teams outside of it.

These are just a few of the many benefits of playing football. As you can see, there are plenty of reasons why people love this sport so much; however, it is important to note that at times there may be certain contraindications that some people may need to take into consideration when making their decision on whether or not they would like to play football. We will now look at some of these.

Contraindications

It is important that you take precautions and make sure you are not putting yourself at risk by wearing gear that will not protect you. It is also important to note that there are a number of reasons why the American Academy of Family Physicians has advised against the participation in full-contact football by children under the age of 14 years. These include:

1. Risk of Injury

While football is a very physical sport, it should not be the cause of or exacerbate pre-existing conditions. If you are prone to injury or have any pre-existing conditions, you should seek a doctor's advice before participating in football. Injuries can occur even when people are wearing helmets, so as with all sports, there is always some risk.

2. Poor Performance

Football players need to be able to concentrate on what they are doing in order to succeed at the sport and do so safely.

This means that it is really important to have good physical conditioning for football. This means the more you play, the better you should get, but having a bad workout can still ruin your performance.

3. Endangerment

The sport of football can actually cause serious injury if players are not careful and not wearing suitable equipment. It is important to note that the Baltimore Ravens lost one of their team members in 2014 when he was playing with a neck injury and suffered a catastrophic spinal cord injury. That player has since passed away.

On the other hand, there have been some injuries that have occurred on the field due to bad equipment such as in 2011 when a player got his leg caught in a scuffle. This resulted in a fracture of the tibia, and he was forced to retire from playing football.

4. Risk of Spinal Cord Injury

While football is a sport that many enjoy, it can also be very dangerous. This can occur due to poor equipment, bad injuries that were not prevented in training or playing, or contact with the ground.

Such bad injuries can cause serious damage to the spinal cord; however, it is possible to prevent this from happening by always wearing suitable gear and taking physical training seriously.

5. Poor Mental Health

Having poor mental health is frequently connected to being in a negative mood, stressed and anxious. This means that poor mental health will affect your performance as well as your ability to concentrate and think clearly while playing.

Playing football may make things worse, leading to more frequent negative thoughts that can lead to stress and anxiety. If you find that you are having a hard time keeping yourself calm, it would be wise for you to stop playing the sport altogether.

Principles And Values of Sports

Sports are just mechanisms for achieving a goal by third parties called teams. Society has developed a lot of norms that encourage participation in sports. For example, the development of physical fitness starts in childhood, with children playing during their free time or engaging in cultural or recreational activities. During this developmental period, the focus is on participating in physical exercise and playing games to develop motor skills and cognitive abilities such as speed and agility. Once these basic motor skills have been developed, they are then introduced into formally structured programs through organized sports.

American football is a game that encourages both physical and mental development. It was first played at an Ivy League school in the United States of America. This meant that it was popularized by well-educated persons who were more focused on intellectual rather than physical pursuits. Because of this, football was not as popular as other games such as soccer and hockey, which made it more challenging to get people interested in the game.

Football has some commonalities with rugby and soccer but also has some differences that make it unique among all other sports.

Chapter 3

TACTICS AND TECHNIQUES

Football is a complex game that has changed significantly since the first Super Bowl was played in 1967. The players, the coaching strategies, and even some rules have all changed to meet new realities. These changes can mean more opportunities for people who want to play football professionally or watch their favourite team.

The game has become more complex as the rules have changed to protect both the players and the fans. Protective equipment has improved, and practice methods that keep players healthy are essential for success in professional football.

Nowadays, a football player must be big and strong, but also fast and agile. An offensive lineman must be able to run downfield, but there is also the need for an offensive lineman who can move quickly on a pass play. The game has changed, and so has the way players are recruited, trained, and developed. The style of play is now faster and more reliant on speed than ever before.

While these developments have added to the intensity of the game and increased its popularity, new coaching strategies have also made it more difficult for people who want to learn about football. They are not just learning about a sport anymore--they are learning about a new way of life for the athletes involved in professional football.

The Use of the Running Back

The running back is one of the most important positions in football. The running back's role in an offense can vary, but they will usually be asked to carry the ball on most plays while also pass-blocking and catching passes out of the backfield.

The use of a running back allows a team to utilize their quarterback better. A good quarterback can only do so much with his arm; having an effective ground game makes it easier for him to find holes in defenses and make plays downfield or across the middle of the field.

Runners also help move chains for offenses by getting first downs when needed or making big gains that result in touchdowns (especially near the red zone).

When running backs break into the open field, a coach experiences the high point of his offense. If a running back has enough speed and agility to break away from multiple defenders and cross the goal line for a touchdown, it can be one of the biggest highlights of an exciting game.

Running Backs in Pass Protection

Sometimes, teams like to throw short routes to their running backs to exploit defences and move the chains. This is an effective strategy for teams that have a strong running game.

When it comes to blocking for these short pass plays, the responsibilities are much different than those of offensive linemen. While linemen must do their jobs on every play and make sure their teammates are safe, running backs are asked to simply protect the quarterback for a few seconds on most plays.

One way to accomplish this is by staying in front of the rusher and turning him back inside toward his own team's line. The running back can also redirect the defender using his hands and body.

Blocking in this capacity isn't as physically demanding, but it is still important for a team to have a good blocker out of the backfield.

Agility, Speed, and Speed of Play

When running broad sweep plays, teams will often try to get their backs outside to see what they can do with the ball. The wide receivers are generally the primary targets on these plays and are asked to run deep routes to try and pick up yards after the catch.

With a wider field to work with, wide receivers can cut inside of a defender and make a big play at the line of scrimmage.

Because they don't have to make tackles, wide receivers can be more creative with their route runs. They don't have the same need for stifling defenders that running backs do, which means they can be more aggressive with their cuts and moves.

The greater emphasis on the running game outside from offensive coordinators has made the wide receiver more of a threat. The increased spacing between defenders has also allowed wide receivers to make plays on their own.

A lot of teams that run an offense like this with a dual-threat quarterback also use two tight ends on most plays, which means they could run sweeps or option plays out of it as well. This is a more advanced tactic that combines the pass and run, but it is still possible in simpler offenses.

Passing Becomes More Dominant

In the modern NFL, passing is a more effective and efficient way to move the ball down the field. Passing has become the dominant offensive strategy in today's NFL. The passing game has grown as teams have adapted their strategies to focus on shorter throws and fewer runs, which allows them to control possession of the ball and score more points than their opponents.

The New England Patriots are one team that has adopted this style of play. Under Bill Belichick's leadership, they've built a team around Tom Brady's skillset by emphasizing short passes over longer runs or throws. This allows them to control possession time but also limits Brady's ability as a runner—which makes sense since he had an ACL injury that ended his college athlete career!

The Players and Their Respective Roles

The best players are often the most productive ones, but they aren't the only ones who are important. In the NFL there are certain roles that the players must fill in order to have success. Offensive linemen, like any other position group, have their own roles to play in order to be an effective offense.

Offensive linemen can be seen at different levels of competition because each offensive line has its own style and set of rules for development and practice. The NFL has a more refined style of play developed over decades of play, whereas college teams may still be developing their rules and styles of play each year.

Offensive Linemen in the NFL

The NFL is unique among professional sports in that it requires its players to be versatile. While offensive linemen may get used to playing a certain spot, they must also learn how to perform at other spots on the line if they are ever called on to do so. Offensive lines are the primary ground for measuring a team's offensive production, which is why players on the line must be able to perform in several different positions.

The Role of the Quarterback

The Quarterback has become the most important position in football. In today's game, it is rare to see teams without a quarterback who can pass accurately and make good decisions with the ball. The quarterback is responsible for calling plays and making adjustments at the line of scrimmage. He or she must be able to throw accurately on short and long throws and have enough athleticism to escape pressure when needed.

When describing what makes a great QB, many people will talk about players like Tom Brady or Aaron Rodgers, who have exceptional arm strength, or guys like Drew Brees, who have pinpoint accuracy. While these qualities are important, they aren't everything! Great quarterbacks must also be able to read defences before making their decision on where they want their offense to go with the ball next.

The modern NFL brings a unique pressure situation. Not only can you be sacked by multiple rushers, but you also have to understand when to hand the ball off to your running back or when to throw a pass. Not many players are able to handle both of these responsibilities at the same time, which is why so many QBs are benched in the fourth quarter.

It's important for a QB to be able to read and react quickly in order to perform at an efficient level.

The Unsung Heros of Defense

Defense can be the most overlooked part of football, but it is just as important as offense. Defense involves more players than offense, and many positions may not get the credit they deserve.

The defensive line consists of:

- Defensive tackles (DTs)

- Nose tackles (NTs)

- Defensive ends (DEs) are responsible for stuffing the run and pressuring the quarterback by eating up blocks so linebackers can make plays in the backfield. They might not get much recognition, but they are essential to a defense's success. Linebackers include inside linebackers (ILBs), outside linebackers (OLBs), and middle linebackers (MLBs). ILBs must be able to drop into coverage against running backs or tight ends, while OLBs need to rush off of their edges on pass-rushing situations. Both ILB and OLB will play different roles depending on if it's a 4-3 or 3-4 defense, but both will still be responsible for stopping running backs from getting past them or attacking quarterbacks from either side if pass rushing.

New Coaching Strategies in the NFL

Coaching strategies are evolving in the NFL. Coaches are using new techniques to get their players to perform better, and they're also using new technology to improve the way they analyze game footage. Some coaches have even started incorporating other sports ideas into their practices as they look for ways to stay ahead of the competition. For example, the Philadelphia Eagles have started using a golf coach to help their players improve their hand-eye coordination and quickness. The New Orleans Saints have also started using a sports psychologist to help their players deal with the stress of playing in front of thousands of fans every Sunday.

Today's players and coaches must be more adaptable than ever before

There are a lot of factors that come into play when talking about the game today. To start with, the players and coaches are just better than they were in previous years. Players have more access to better training facilities and coaching staff. This means they can adapt their techniques much quicker than in years past. Coaches also have access to more advanced technology and better tools for analyzing their own players, allowing them to make adjustments based on what they see in practice or during games.

As teams continue to get better at developing talent and building solid rosters, it's important for coaches to keep up with this trend by finding new ways to stay ahead of their counterparts around the league. Many teams do this by bringing in new offensive coordinators who bring fresh ideas from other leagues or coaches from other teams who may have been able to find success through unique strategies not yet tried by others at this level (like Rob Chudzinski).

The game of football is constantly evolving and changing, so it's important for coaches and players to stay one step ahead. These tactics and techniques help keep things fresh in a sport that has been around for over 100 years but still manages to captivate millions every year.

Football Terms to Make You Sound Like A Pro

If you know at least a little about American football, you probably know what the words run, pass, and touchdown means. However, if terminology like blitz, pick six, muff, and squib kick are sacking you, call an audible and gather up our dictionary of football terms that will send your understanding of pigskin straight through the uprights. You'll be able to talk about football like a coach on the sidelines with these football terms and phrases.

Audible: the changing of the play by the QB before the snap, communicated through code words and hands signals

Back: an offensive player who lines up behind the line of scrimmage, i.e. quarterback, halfback, running back

Backfield: the area behind the offense's LOS. Also refers to the players themselves in the backfield.

Ball carrier: the player currently in possession of a live ball

Ball security: the skill of holding onto the ball at all costs and preventing fumbles

Blitz: a defensive maneuver in which five or more players rush the quarterback. Usually a linebacker or defensive back is the extra pass rusher.

Blocking: actively obstructing the path of another player

Bootleg play: the quarterback runs out of the pocket toward the sideline, then passes or runs downfield

Bubble screen: an offensive play in which a wide receiver receives the ball behind the LOS while the other receivers block for him

Bump and run: a defensive technique in which the DB tries to bump or quickly push the receiver to throw him off his route

Bye week: a scheduled week off for a team during the regular season

Catch: the act of receiving a pass, which must satisfy the three conditions of 1) control, 2) planting two feet (or another body part) down in bounds, and 3) the receiver making a "football move"

Catch and run: when a running back or receiver catches a pass and then immediately turns to run downfield with the ball

Challenge flag: a red cloth marker that a coach uses to signal that he disagrees with the result of the previous play and is requesting that the officials take another look in instant replay

Checkdown pass: a short, last-resort pass to a running back or tight end if the quarterback's primary targets can't get open

Clock management: strategically manipulating the game clock, especially at the end of the game

Conversion: another way to say "getting a first down." Also refers to the PAT attempt.

Cornerback (CB): a defensive back player who mostly covers receivers and can also be responsible for stopping running plays

Coverage shells: the scheme used for zone passing coverage

Dead ball: the status of the football not currently in play (between plays, ball goes out of bounds, incomplete pass is thrown)

Defense: the team trying to stop the offense from scoring, and the methods that they use to accomplish this

Defensive back (DB): a cornerback or safety, part of the secondary

Defensive end (DE): a defensive lineman on the edge of the formation who stops end runs as well as rushes the quarterback on passing plays

Defensive line: the players who begin downs on the line of scrimmage, responsible for both run and pass protection. Defensive tackles and defensive ends are both defensive linemen.

defensive tackle (DT): a defensive lineman on the interior of the formation who can be called upon to stop running plays or pressure the quarterback

Double-team: when two players cover or block an opposing player

Down: 1) an attempt for the offense to reach its line to gain, i.e. "third down" 2) the status of a player once any part of his body except his hands or feet touches the field and is contacted by another player

Down lineman: any offensive or defensive lineman in a 3-point or 4-point stance

Downfield: a reference point to indicate in front of the offense and behind the defense

Draft bust: a player selected high in the NFL draft who underperforms in the league

Draft steal: a player who is passed in the draft by many teams, but later performs far beyond his expectations in the NFL

Draw: the mirror of a play-action play. The QB fakes a passing play, but hands it off to a running back.

Dual-threat/mobile quarterbacks: quarterbacks who are equally skilled at passing the ball and running with it himself

End line: the line marking the back of the end zone

End run: a play in which ball carrier (usually a running back) runs around the end of the linemen

End zones: the two areas at both ends of the field where all the scoring happens

Expansion team: a new team added to the NFL

Extra point attempt: a PAT attempt from the 15-yard line, made by kicking the ball through the uprights

Fair catch: a signal made by the kick or punt returner, indicating to the other team that he will not attempt to return the ball

Field of play: the 100-yard by 53 ▢-yard area where the game is played

Field position: the location of the offense on the field

First down: the reward for the offense if they advance 10 yards closer to the opponent's end zone within four downs. Also automatically given to the offense after a turnover or scoring play.

Flag: a weighted yellow penalty marker to indicate that a foul has occurred during the play

Flanker/Z-receiver: a wide receiver who lines up behind the LOS, usually on the strong side of the formation

Foul/penalty: a violation of NFL rules during the game

Free safety (FS): a defensive back who lines up on the weak side of the formation. Responsible for both run and deep pass protection.

Fullback (FB): a position in the offensive backfield who serves as a blocker but also sometimes runs with the ball

Fumble: the ball carrier loses control of a live ball by dropping it, or has it punched or pried out of his hands

Fumble recovery: gain possession of a fumbled live ball

Gap: a hole between the offensive linemen

Goal line: the line that separates the field of play from the end zone

Goalpost/upright: one of two yellow poles that indicate where the ball must be kicked in order to score points

Gunners: special teams players on punting/kickoff plays who chase the returner and try to tackle him

H-back: an offensive player who is a fullback/tight end hybrid. A de facto tight end that plays behind the LOS instead of on it.

Hail Mary: a very long passing play when there is little or no time left in the game

Halfback (see running back)

Halftime: a 12-minute break between the 2nd and 3rd quarters

Handoff: the process of the quarterback stuffing the ball into a running back's arms on running plays

Hang time: how long the ball stays airborne after a punt

Hard count: a technique used by quarterbacks to fool the defense into thinking the ball has been snapped and to get them to jump offsides

Hash marks: vertical columns of white lines used for spotting the ball

Hike (see snap)

Holder: a special teams player in charge of receiving the snap and holding the ball for the placekicker during field goal attempts and extra point tries. Holders are often backup quarterbacks or other "good hands" players.

Hot receiver: a receiver designated ahead of time to catch a short pass from the QB if told to do so through an audible, in response to a problematic defensive formation

Huddle: the gathering of the offense to plan and discuss the next play

Hurry: when the quarterback is pressured by the defense and is forced to throw or scramble to avoid a sack

Hurry-up/no-huddle offense: an offensive strategy to conserve time on the game clock and/or preserve momentum

Icing the kicker: the defense calls a timeout before a kicking play in an attempt to make the kicker nervous and hopefully miss

Incomplete pass: a pass that is not caught by any player

Injured reserve (IR): a roster designation for players who are hurt and normally unable to return for the remainder of the regular season

Instant replay: showing the previous play again in slow motion, for the benefit of fans watching on television as well as the officials during play reviews

Intentional grounding: the QB throws the ball in an area where there are no receivers, and while he is still in the pocket (usually to avoid a sack)

Interception/"pick": a forward pass that is caught by a defensive player instead of the targeted receiver

Jam the receiver: a blocking technique used by defensive backs to slow down their assigned receiver

Jammers: special teams players from the receiving team on kickoff plays who try to slow down the gunners

Juking: faking out defenders by pretending to move in one direction and then suddenly changing course

Kicker (see placekicker)

Kickoff: a free kicking play to start off the 1st and 3rd quarters, as well as the play immediately after a team score

Kick returner: a special teams player who waits at the opposite side of the field during kickoff, and then returns the ball toward the opponent's end zone

Lateral/backward pass: a pass thrown in line with the LOS or away from it

Lead blocking: a technique typically used by an offensive lineman or fullback, when he gets in front of the running back to clear defenders out of his way

Linebackers: the defensive players behind the defensive linemen, responsible for both pass and run protection

Line of scrimmage (LOS): the imaginary line separating the offense and defense, which may not be crossed until the ball is snapped

Line to gain: an imaginary line that marks the point where the offense needs to travel in order to get a first down

Lockdown/shutdown corner: an exceptional cornerback who rarely allows the quarterback to complete a pass to the receiver covered by that corner

Long snapper: a special teams player who snaps the ball to the punter or ball holder

Man block: an offensive line strategy in which the linemen commit to blocking an assigned defender everywhere he goes

Man coverage: a defensive strategy in which each defender is individually responsible for following and covering offensive player

Middle linebacker (MLB): also known as the "Mike," and can be thought of as the quarterback of the defense

Motion: an offensive player changing their position in the formation during the snap

National Football League (NFL): the dominant professional American gridiron football league

NFL Draft: the primary means for teams to select players who are finished with their college football careers

Nickelback/nickel: a fifth defensive back placed on or near the LOS in place of the weak side linebacker

Non-Football Injury (NFI) list: a roster designation similar to the PUP list, for players injured in way unrelated to football

Nose tackle (NT): the single defensive tackle in a 3-4 defense

Offense: the team currently in control of the ball, trying to score

Officials/"zebras": the referee and line judges

Onside kick: a short kickoff used as a desperation play to try and regain ball possession

Option offense: an offensive scheme that allows for a passing or running play after the snap, based on the actions of the defense

Outside linebackers (OLBs): one of two linebackers in a defensive formation, including the "Sam" and "Will" positions

Package: another name for a defensive substitution personnel group, such as the nickel or dime defense

Pancake block: a perfect block, in which the defender is pushed backward and ends up lying flat on his back, while the blocker remains standing

Pass coverage: the actions taken by the defense to make sure receivers do not catch a pass from the quarterback, e.g. man/zone coverage

Pass protection: the job of offensive linemen to block defenders from rushing and/or sacking the quarterback during a passing play

Pass rush: the efforts by the defense to pressure the quarterback and stop him from throwing a completed pass

Passing pocket: the tackle box on the offensive side of the LOS, where the QB stands to look for a receiver

Passing route/pattern: the directional pattern that a receiver follows after the snap

Penalty (see fouls)

Personnel grouping: describes the positional makeup of the 11 players currently on the field. Can also be called a package, such as a "goal line package" or "nickel package."

Physically unable to perform (PUP) list: a roster designation for players who have an injury from the previous season or a preseason game

Pick (see interception)

Pick-6: an interception returned for a touchdown by the defensive team

Pistol formation: an offensive formation in which the QB lines up about three yards behind the center

Placekicker/kicker: an exclusively special teams player who kicks the ball through the uprights for field goals and extra point attempts, as well as begins the 1st and 3rd quarters with the kickoff

Play: the action that occurs between the snap and when the ball becomes dead. A play also refers to different types of planned strategies, such as a running or passing play.

Play-action pass: technically a trick play, in which the QB fakes handing the ball off but then drops back to pass

Point(s) after touchdown (P.A.T.) attempt: the chance for a team to earn either 1 point (extra point attempt) or 2 points (2-point conversion) after a touchdown

Pop Warner: a youth football league for kids aged 5-16 years old

Possession: currently in physical control of the ball, or in control of the ball by virtue of being the team on offense

Postseason: the playoffs, a series of single-elimination games that eventually determines the NFL world champion in the Super Bowl

Practice squad: the most junior roster position, reserved for players who only participate in practice, but not actual games

Preseason: the 4-week stretch of exhibition games in which rookies and other non-starter players get a chance to earn their place on the final roster

Prevent defense: a defensive strategy designed to stop long passes at the expense of possibly giving up short passes

Pro Bowl: the annual "All-Star" exhibition game between the best players in the league, as selected by NFL players, coaches, and fans

Pro Football Hall of Fame: a select group of players recognized for their outstanding contribution to the game

Pump fake: a quick passing motion by the quarterback to get the defense to think he's going to pass, only to hold onto the ball and then pass on the next motion

Punt returner: a special teams player who waits downfield for a punted ball, and runs with it as long as possible toward the opponent's end zone

Punter: a special teams player who receives the ball from the long snapper, and then drops and kicks the ball high into the air and down the field

Pylon: one of four orange markers at the corners of each end zone

Quarterback: an offensive player in the backfield that passes or hands off the ball, calls out Plays and adjustments, and serves as a leader of the team

Quarterback kneel/victory formation: an offensive formation used by the winning team at the end of the game, in which the quarterback takes a knee to run down the game clock safely

Read option/zone read: part of the option offense. A play in which the offensive linemen attempt to push all defenders in one direction during the handoff to a running back. The QB then reads the defense and decides whether to finish the handoff.

Receiver: an offensive player who catches passes from the quarterback

Reception: a successful catch of a pass

Red zone: the area of the field within 20 yards of the opponent's end zone

Referee: the head of the other officials

Regular season: the 17-week period in which NFL games are played from September to December to determine who advances to the postseason

Released: cut from the roster by a team

Rookies: first-year players

Route (see passing route)

Run protection: the act of blocking defenders and clearing a hole for a running back to run through. Generally performed by the offensive line.

Running back: an offensive player in the backfield that receives handoffs on running plays and sometimes short passes from the QB

Rushing attempt/"carry": a play in which any player (normally a running back or the quarterback) attempts to run with the ball to gain yards

Sack: a play in which the quarterback is tackled behind the line of scrimmage

Safety (scoring play): a two-point score, awarded when 1) the ball carrier is tackled in his own end zone, 2) the ball carrier is forced out of bounds while in the end zone by the opposing team, or 3) the defense forces the ball carrier to fumble the ball out of the end zone

Salary cap: the total amount of money a team is permitted to pay its players

Sam linebacker: the linebacker who plays on the strong side of the formation

Scat back: a quick and evasive halfback, on the smaller side

Scheme: the overall strategy the offense or defense is currently using

Scout: a representative of NFL and college teams who look for talented players to bring to their organization or school

Scouting combine: an invitation-only event for college players to be evaluated by NFL team scouts

Scramble: an improvised run with the ball by the quarterback

Screen pass: a play in which a receiver catches a pass behind the LOS while protected by a wall (screen) of blockers

Seam: the area where the zone coverage responsibilities of defenders meet

Secondary: the area occupied by the defensive backs, or the DBs themselves

Separation: the space between an offensive and defensive player, i.e. a situation in which an O-lineman attempts to gain leverage on the defender or a receiver tries to put enough distance between himself and a defender in order to get open for a pass

Set: the status of the offense when they stop moving for at least one second prior to the snap, as required

Shift: one or more offensive players changes position before the snap

Shoot the gap: a defensive lineman tries to squeeze through the space between offensive linemen to get to the quarterback

Shotgun formation: the quarterback receives the snap about five yards behind the center

Shovel pass: a quick underhand toss to another player

Sideline: the border around the field of play

Single-back set: an offensive formation in which the QB is under center, and a single running back is lined up about five yards behind the QB

Skill positions: all positions except the offensive and defensive linemen

Slot receiver/slotback: the receiver lined up between the X or Z receiver and an offensive tackle

Snap/hike: when the center puts the ball into play by throwing it backward between his legs to another player, usually the quarterback

Special teams: a group of players used during kickoffs, punts, field goal tries, and extra point tries. Includes players from the offense and defense as well as exclusively special teams players.

Spike: when the quarterback receives the snap and immediately throws it to the ground in order to stop the clock

Split end/"X-receiver": a wide receiver on the LOS lined up on the weak side of the formation

Spot: the placement of the ball in its position for the start of the next play

Spread offense: an offensive strategy in which the QB is in the shotgun and there are 3-5 receivers lined up in the formation

Squib kick: a short kickoff designed to prevent a big return by the receiving team

stacking the box: a defensive strategy that puts one or more extra defenders into the tackle box for increased run protection

starters: the best players at their position on the team

Stiff-arm: an offensive technique used by the ball carrier to ward off tacklers. He extends his straight, locked arm into the defender's chest or shoulder.

Strip sack: a defender forces a fumble during a sack

Strong safety (SS): a defensive back who lines up on the same side as the tight end. Used primarily for pass coverage.

Strong side: the side of the formation containing the tight end

Subpackage: a personnel grouping other than a base defense, one with more or less than four defensive backs on the field at any given time

Super Bowl: the championship game of the NFL, between the AFC and NFC champions

Tackle: any physical method a defensive player uses to bring down the ball carrier or stop his forward progress

Tackle box: the area between the offensive linemen and within five yards or so from the line of scrimmage

Tackle for loss (TFL): a tackle behind the LOS, resulting in the loss of yards for the offense (moving their line to gain further away)

Tailback: another name for a halfback, describing his position at the rear of the formation

Technique: a positional term for the location of defensive linemen in relation to the offensive linemen

Three and out: a situation in which a team was not able to achieve a first down within three tries, and uses their fourth down to punt

Tight end: the Y-receiver lined up directly next to an offensive tackle

Time of possession: a statistic that keeps track of how much time a team spent in control of the ball (on offense)

Timeout: a two-minute break that can be called by either head coach or any player on the field. Three timeouts are given to each team for each half of the game.

Total defense: the total amount of yards a team allowed the offense to gain during the game (the smaller the number, the better the defense)

Total offense: the total amount of yards a team gained during the course of the game (the larger the number, the better the offense)

Touchback: a result of a play (such as a kickoff or punt) when the ball becomes dead in the defensive team's end zone (or goes out of bounds in the end zone) and the offensive team was the last to touch the ball

Touchdown: a scoring play worth six points, earned by gaining possession of the ball in his opponent's end zone or crossing the plane of the goal line with the ball

Trick plays: exotic/out of the ordinary plays meant to confuse or throw off the defense

Trips formation: a formation with three receivers on one side of the offensive line

Try (see P.A.T. attempt)

Turnover: a change of ball possession. Also called a takeaway if the turnover is the result of an interception or a fumble recovery by the defense.

Two-minute warning: a four-minute timeout for both teams when there is two minutes remaining in the 2nd and 4th quarters

Two-point conversion: a PAT attempt from the 2-yard line, completed by the offense gaining possession of the ball in the end zone

Under center: the positioning of the quarterback when he is directly behind the center before the snap

Upfield: a reference point to indicate the area behind the offense and in front of the defense

Victory formation (see quarterback kneel)

Weak side: the side of the offensive formation without a tight end

West coast offense: an offensive scheme that relies on short passing plays with a high rate of completion

Wild cards: two teams from each conference with the best regular season record that did not win their divisions teams. The lowest seeded teams in the playoffs.

Will linebacker: the linebacker that plays on the weak side of the formation

Y receiver: a receiver that can be a slot receiver or a tight end

Z receiver (see flanker)

Zone blitz: a defensive maneuver in which the apparent pass rushers (the D-linemen) drop back into pass coverage, while the linebackers/DBs take on the role of pressuring the QB

Zone block: an offensive line strategy in which linemen block defenders in a specific area, rather than specific defenders themselves

Zone coverage: a defensive pass coverage strategy, in which defenders are assigned to protect areas of the field from pass completions

Chapter 4

THE NATIONAL FOOTBALL LEAGUE (NFL)

NFL, often known as American football, has gained popularity in the United States of America and is frequently viewed by fans of the game as a superior alternative to rugby or soccer. Because of the prohibitions on touchdown celebrations, strong hits, and tackles, non-sports viewers frequently refer to the league as "No Fun League" or "Not For Long," which alludes to the average player's brief career in the league. In summary, the NFL should be given greater credit for its economic impact and level of activity.

The National Football League's annual revenue of over $1 billion, which represents a significant portion of the sport, is well known. The average NFL club is worth over $3 billion, according to a Forbes appraisal. The NFL brand has proven to be quite successful, with matches even taking place in Mexico City and London, England. The average number of viewers for NFL regular season games on TV in 2018 increased over the previous year by 5%.

History of the NFL

On September 17, 1920, owners of existing professional football teams gathered to organize the American Professional Football Association (APFA) at a Hupmobile showroom in Canton, Ohio. It's unlikely that George Halas and the other signees could have foreseen that the APFA would transform into the National Football League two years later (NFL). Red Grange, the first major NFL star, was soon up and running. In 1925, he ran from the campus of Illinois to the Bears and the Bank, pocketing the awful sum of $100,000, to excite throngs of spectators as galloping ghosts.

The NFL established the NFL championship game, played between the top teams in each division, in 1933 to take advantage of its growing popularity. At the time, teams like the Tim Maris Giants and the Redskins, led by Sling and Sammy Baugh (who lived up to his name by tossing the ball all over the gridiron), were formidable foes for the Granges Bears, who participated in seven of the first eleven championship games.

The NFL suffered greatly from World War II in 1939, just like the rest of America. Due to the depletion of two league rosters, two teams were merged. For instance, whoever was left faced up against the Steagles. When the soldiers returned home, though, football had grown in popularity enough to establish a second league, the AAFC, which featured groups like the Browns, 49ers, and Colts. The two leagues amalgamated in 1949, saving the sport from being killed by rivalry.

Coach Paul Brown contributed innovation and dominance to the NFL along with his Browns. In the 1950s, he was the first coach to advocate for film study, which contributed to three victories. Detroit was succeeding if the Browns weren't. Bobby Lane as the quarterback helped them win three times. In what is widely regarded as the greatest game ever played, Johnny Unitas helped the Colts pull off an incredible comeback victory in sudden death overtime to cap off the decade.

The AFL and teams like the Bills, Broncos, Chargers, Chiefs, Oilers, and Raiders were both created as a result of the enormous demand for football. But in the NFL, the Cotton Bowl and the first two Super Bowls saw only the Packers win championships. When the league's championship trophy was given the Vince Lombardi name in honor of their head coach, their legendary position was cemented. Jim Brown continued to shatter records until he finally retired at the ripe old age of 29. Broadway Joe's assurance of a Jets triumph in Super Bowl 3 stole the show. Fans realized AFL teams were no longer major factors when they successfully upset the Colts, as they had promised.

The NFL and AFL combined their ground-and-pound football systems in 1970. From the Electric Company to the newly crowned champions, the Dolphins, who grounded out two championships, the run game was in favor. Tom Lnadry's

Cowboys also did. These Cowboys and their cheerleaders earned themselves a new moniker, the title of America's team, and two Super Bowl victories thanks to Dwanye the Silent, Tony D, and the "Doomsday" defense. With their two jacks, a mean Joe, and a swan dive, the Steelers Trump ruled the 1970s as well.

There were some handoffs during the disco era thanks to a quarterback with a mustache and a smart coach who invented the "Air Coryell" supercharged modern offense. San Diego may not have taken home a Lombardi, but they were noticed by the Walshes and Parcells. San Francisco scored three times thanks to Walsh's blast past the West Coast offensive. Parcell, who has won two Super Bowls, though, set his sights on neutralizing it and any other wide-open offensive. While everything was going on, Gibbs won the Redskins three championships before he left Coryell's coaching staff and returned to the field.

Reggie White joined Green Bay and helped the Packers win their third Super Bowl, much like their opponents in Dallas, who were led by a colorful owner and won the Lombardi trophy three times in the early 1990s. While all of that was going on, Jerry Rice broke numerous records and the Bills lost four Super Bowls, which set a new standard for fan annoyance. In a different trick, Terrel Davis and John Elway won two championships despite having a migraine. The Music City miracle then turned out to be just a sneak peek of the biggest event on Turf.

The previous powerhouses were disintegrating as the league entered the 2000s due to the tag Limu salary cap and parody period, making room for fresh winners like the Ravens and Buccaneers. The beginning of the era's first true dynasty was defined by a backup quarterback teaming up with a scruffy genius. The matches against Peyton Manning are renowned in the sport. Brady would be foiled by the other Manning, and David Tyree would show that being a big player can pay off.

Ben Roethlisberger also made sure that Steelers supporters received a ring for their thumb and other hand. No team from this decade has beaten the odds, unlike the 20s. In the subsequent game, Brees moated Beiste while still saving the Saints. With the lights on or off, the scorching-hot Ravens were unable to refuel, and the squad that was one yard away from repeating had its hopes dashed at the goal line. With more than 100 seasons, the NFL has advanced considerably. Who would have imagined that a Hupmobile dealership could propel an NFL team all the way to the Super Bowl.

Organization of the NFL

Currently, there are 32 teams in the NFL, spread out across the country. The American Football Conference (AFC) and the National Football Conference are the two conferences that separate them (NFC). The 16 teams are evenly distributed throughout these conferences' four divisions, each of which corresponds to a compass's north, south, east, and west axes.

On a grass or turf field that is 120 yards long and 53.3 yards wide, American football is played. End zones, which are 10 yards long and where teams can score, are on either side of the field. The remainder of the field is marked with lines every five yards and hash marks every yard. Goal posts that are 10 feet tall and 18 feet 6 inches wide are located behind each end zone.

The game lasts a total of 60 minutes, which are broken up into four 15-minute quarters. A 12-minute halftime is used between the second and third quarters to give teams time to reorganize. The NFL has a 10-minute overtime phase to determine who will win if the score is tied at the end of regular. A game is deemed a tie if both teams receive the same score.

Additionally, the NFL's regular season runs from the beginning of September until the end of December. All 32 clubs in the league play 16 games each over the 256-game schedule, which is stretched out over a period of 17 weeks. Each team also has a bye week, which is a day off for fans and sports enthusiasts. The NFL hierarchy came up with a method for scheduling the league because each team cannot play the other 31 teams all at once, unlike in other professional sports.

The Cleveland Browns will be used as an example to demonstrate how the NFL formula works. The Browns will first play six games — one at home and one away – against opponents from their division. The Browns will then play four games, two at home and two away, against a different Division within the same Conference. The Browns will then play four more games—two at home and two away—against a different Division but outside of a Conference. Finally, the final two games are against opponents from the Conference's final two Divisions.

These meetings are chosen based on the Division standings from the previous year. For instance, the Browns would face the fourth club in both of those Divisions if they had finished fourth the previous season. Every team will play each of the 31 teams at least once throughout a four-year period because the schedule rotates each year.

The single elimination postseason, which follows the regular season, starts in early January and finishes in February with the Super Bowl, the last game. Six teams from each Conference make up the 12 teams that can compete. The four divisional champions as well as the two wild card teams make up the bracket. The two non-Divisional champions with the best overall record in the Conference are the Wild Card teams.

Let's take the 2018 postseason as an example to show how the postseason placement functions. Whoever has a better record among the four Divisional champions receives the 1–4 ranking. While the #3 and #4 play their respective Wild Card opponent, the #1 and #2 have a bye week. The winner of the two contests advances to the divisional stage, where it will face the winner of the lower seed. Before the highly anticipated Super Bowl game, this then advances to the Conference championship game. The NFL season for that year comes to a conclusion when the Super Bowl champion is announced.

Top Players of All Time

After talking about the greatest franchises of all time, it is time to examine the greatest players of all time as individuals. It is now much harder to select the best players in a sport like football than it is in a sport like basketball or hockey. Why? because there are three very distinct playing divisions in the NFL. There are special teams in addition to the offense, defense, and special teams. A top player across all three aspects of the game must be chosen because none of the game's components is "more significant" than the others. In the NBA, for example, every player on the court is required to play both offense and defense at once. The NFL has established offense and defensive positions!

In spite of this, it is still possible to go position by position and examine some of the finest performers in the field's history. In this chapter, we'll carry it out. This chapter is going to do a deep dive into each position and select out some of the best to ever put on a chinstrap, from the flashiest quarterbacks to the gritty offensive lineman! I'm hoping you share my enthusiasm.

The Top Players of All Time at Each Position

Quarterback: It seems only right to start with the position that gets the most flair. In no particular order, here are the greatest quarterbacks to ever play the game.

Troy Aikman (1989–2000) Played for the Dallas Cowboys: Compared to some of the other players on this list, Troy Aikman may seem like a bit of an odd addition. Why? Well, there was nothing he did that was particularly flashy, especially when compared to his teammates Emmitt Smith and Michael Irvin. Aikman was often overshadowed by those two teammates. Smith and Irvin are both Hall of Famers who were the very best at what a running back and receiver duo could offer. Thus, the quarterback of the Cowboys in this era, Aikman, probably didn't get the recognition he deserved. This is a little cheap because what Aikman did on the field as a leader and player put him among the best to ever do it at the quarterback position. He was poised, calm, cool, and confident—all traits you want in your quarterback. While his stats are nowhere near as impressive as a Tom Brady or Peyton Manning, Aikman was still able to guide his Cowboys to three Super Bowl victories in just 11 seasons. He was accurate with the ball, made smart decisions, and almost always got his team in a position to potentially win football games. Like all great players, he seemed to play his most confident football when it mattered most. He was 3-0 in the Super Bowl and threw a total of five touchdowns and just one interception in those three games.

Joe Montana (1979–1994) Played for the San Francisco 49ers and Kansas City Chiefs: Joe Montana was so special because he always seemed to play his best football when it mattered the most. Owning four Super Bowl trophies and three Super Bowl Most Valuable Player (MVP) awards, Montana shone the brightest when the lights were on him. He also has the fabulous distinction of never losing a Super Bowl game (4-0). The prototype for all players hoping to make it in the NFL, cool Joe was a special talent. Another important fact about Joe: He was the player who Tom Brady idolized growing up. If Montana wasn't as special a player, maybe the NFL world would've never been given the gift of Tom Brady... something to think about!

Otto Graham (1946–1955) Played for the Cleveland Browns: One of the forgotten legends to play the game, Otto Graham was a three-time NFL champion for the Browns back in the mid-1940s to mid-1950s. A quarterback who truly revolutionized the game with his mix of running and passing, Graham is one of the greatest Cleveland Browns in NFL history. He was inducted into the Hall of Fame in 1965 and was a five-time pro bowler. Quick note, the Pro Bowl is something that happens every year and invites the best players from the regular season from all teams to compete in an All-Star Game. It is considered a high honor, though not as high as a spot in the Hall of Fame!

Peyton Manning (1998–2015) Played for the Indianapolis Colts and Denver Broncos: One of Tom Brady's greatest rivals, Peyton Manning was a phenomenal quarterback who put up some of the greatest statistical seasons of all time. On top of that, he also won two Super Bowls, five MVPs, and has multiple records for passing yards, touchdowns, and other accolades. His greatest accolade likely came in 2013 with the Denver Broncos. That season, he threw for 55 touchdowns and close to 5,500 yards! Those numbers are simply incredible and average out to over three touchdowns a game!

Johnny Unitas (1955–1973) Played for the Pittsburgh Steelers, Baltimore Colts, and San Diego Chargers: Another Colts quarterback making an appearance, here. A Hall of Fame quarterback and four-time NFL champion, Johnny Unitas helped open the door for the Peyton Manning's and Troy Aikman's of the NFL. With the nickname "the Golden Arm," it is not surprising that Unitas held onto the record for most games with a touchdown pass until it was broken by Drew Brees in 2012. That record stood for over 50 years! Fundamental, tough, and incredibly talented, Unitas is considered by many to be the first great quarterback.

Though he no longer plays for the New England Patriots, Tom Brady will forever be known as a Boston legend. He is one of the most beloved athletes in the history of the sports-rich city, even though he now plays for the Tampa Bay Buccaneers.

Tom Brady (2000–Present) Played for the New England Patriots and Tampa Bay Buccaneers: I know I said this list was going to be in no particular order, but there is a reason why Tom Brady is going last for the quarterbacks. He is practically the undisputed Greatest of All Time at the position, winning more Super Bowls (7) than any other franchise has (NFL titles excluded). Those are simply astounding numbers. The craziest part? He is still doing it today. Despite being in the league for over two decades, Brady is currently leading the entire NFL in passing yards at the time of this book. While he has undoubtedly been surrounded by great coaches, players, and defenses in his career, that doesn't change the fact that Brady is the best quarterback in history. He's a three-time MVP and 13-time Pro-Bowler. The guy is simply unstoppable and is going to be inducted into the Hall of Fame shortly after he retires.

Running Backs

Barry Sanders (1989–1998) Played for the Detroit Lions: Another running back who had a relatively short career, Barry Sanders was one of the most electrifying players to ever step onto a football field. Considered by many to be the best player to never appear in a Super Bowl, Sanders still earned one league MVP, four trips to the Pro Bowl, and a Hall of Fame induction in 2004. While not a particularly tall or strong man, Sanders used incredible speed, footwork, and skills to move around, through, and even over defenders! In all 10 seasons that he played, he was always a 1,000-yard rusher. Simply put, he was a once-in-a-generation talent.

Emmitt Smith (1990–2004) Played for the Dallas Cowboys: Even with other Hall of Famers Troy Aikman and Michael Irvin stealing touches away from him, Emmitt Smith was still a dominant presence in the Dallas Cowboys offense for over a decade. Owning an MVP award, one Super Bowl MVP, and a spot in the Hall of Fame, Emmitt Smith was nearly unstoppable behind a great Cowboys offensive line. His best season came in 1995 when he rushed for over 1,700 yards, added over 350 more receiving yards, and accounted for 25 total touchdowns! All of those stats are incredible, and so was Emmitt...he is one of the best running backs to ever play the game.

Walter Payton (1975–1987) Played for the Chicago Bears: While Gale Sayers may have set the stage for great Chicago running backs, Walter Payton took the idea and ran with it—literally! He is one of the most consistent running backs of all time, earning a place in the Hall of Fame, while also sporting an MVP and Super Bowl MVP trophy, too. His best season likely came in 1977 when he ran for over 1,800 yards and scored 20 touchdowns. Slick, strong, tough, and fast, it took a whole army to bring this guy down once he got into the open field. As good a man off the field as he was a player on the field, the league eventually created the Walter Payton Man of the Year Award. Considered to be one of the most prestigious honors in the NFL, it is awarded to a player who shows exemplary service off the field.

Jim Brown (1957–1965) Played for the Cleveland Browns: Much like Tom Brady and the list of quarterbacks, though I claimed that the list was in no particular order, it is pretty clear that Jim Brown is the best running back to ever play the game. He's a Hall of Famer, won a Super Bowl, was a three-time MVP, and was simply one of the toughest players to ever put on an NFL jersey. His best season came in 1963 when he accounted for over 2,000 all-purpose yards and 15 touchdowns. Stronger than arguably any other player to ever play the position and with speed to boot, Jim Brown is one of the few players in NFL history that you can confidently say would be able to dominate regardless of the era in which he played.

Jerry Rice (1985–2004): Played for the San Francisco 49ers, Oakland Raiders, and Seattle Seahawks: Considered by many to be the second-best offensive player of all time, Jerry Rice won an incredible three Super Bowls alongside his quarterback, Joe Montana, for the San Francisco 49ers. He had some of his best seasons of all time with the 49ers, with his best, in particular, coming in 1995. That year, he recorded over 1,800 receiving yards to go with 15 touchdowns. Big, consistent, tough, and clutch beyond all belief, Jerry Rice was near unguardable whether he was playing with Montana or any other quarterback. He was simply a special talent.

Tight End

Tony Gonalez (1997–2013): Played for the Kansas City Chiefs and Atlanta Falcons: The greatest tight end of all time is undoubtedly Tony Gonzalez. A great blocker, pass-catcher, and runner of the football, Gonzales was nearly unstoppable and was massively influential in ushering in a new type of tight end to the game. Before Gonzalez, tight ends were historically blocking players and little more. They would occasionally catch a pass, yes, but their number one priority was opening lanes for the running back to run through. Gonzalez changed that. His best season was likely in 2000 as a member of the Kansas City Chiefs. That season, he caught over 1,200 yards and scored 9 touchdowns. Before him, those numbers would only be seen in wide receivers! A great man on and off the field, Gonzalez was inducted into the Hall of Fame in 2019. Despite never winning a Super Bowl, Gonzalez remains one of the best to ever do it at the tight end position.

Offensive Line

Forrest Gregg (1956–1971) Played for the Green Bay Packers and Dallas Cowboys: Though offensive linemen never get the same glory as the rest of the offensive players around them, doing anything on offense without these behemoths protecting your quarterback would be impossible. Forrest Gregg, a Hall of Famer and staple of Vince Lombardi's Super Bowl-winning teams, was excellent as both a pass protector and run blocker. He won a total of eight championships stretching from the pre-merger until the early 70s. For those counting at home...yes! That is one more than Tom Brady has won.

Defense

Linebacker:

Lawrence Taylor (1981-1993) Played for the New York Giants: Not only is Lawrence Taylor the greatest linebacker of all time, but he is also likely the greatest defensive player of all time. Epitomizing the phrase "defense wins championships," Taylor was one of the toughest guys to cover in the history of the game. Fast, powerful, and tough, Taylor made it difficult for any offensive lineman to have a chance working against him. He won two championships with the Giants, with his best season likely coming in 1986 when he was able to record 20.5 sacks! While the half-sack stat may look odd for some of you, it is important to note that players can share sacks if they both get to the quarterback. Labeled as likely the hardest-hitting player in history, Lawrence Taylor was one player you didn't want to cross.

Defensive End:

Reggie White (1985–2000) Played for the Philadelphia Eagles, Green Bay Packers, and Carolina Panthers: Another player who was awesome at getting after the quarterback, many consider Reggie White to be the greatest pass-rusher of all time. At such a violent position, it takes a special kind of toughness to power through the daily grind and continue to get after the quarterback. That was Reggie White. Relentless, fast, and powerful, Reggie White was able to get past almost any lineman and alter the quarterback's plan. His best season came in 1987 when he was able to record 21.0 sacks for the Philadelphia Eagles. A Super Bowl champion, defensive player of the year, and Hall of Famer, Reggie White was able to do it all in his 14-year career.

Defensive Tackle:

Joe Greene (1969–1981) Played for the Pittsburgh Steelers: Anybody with the nickname "Mean" Joe Greene has to be considered one of the best defensive players of all time, right? In Joe Greene's case...yes! A four-time Super Bowl champion with the Pittsburgh Steelers, Joe Green helped set the tone for that amazing line of defenses in Pittsburgh. In other words, he was the main reason behind the Steelers nickname for those seasons: The Steel Curtain. His best season likely came in 1972 when he was able to record 11 sacks to go along with being one of the toughest run stoppers in the league. A no-doubt Hall of Famer and brutal competitor, Joe Greene helped pave the way for the modern-day defensive tackle.

Safety:

Ronnie Lott (1981–1994) Played for the San Francisco 49ers, Los Angeles Raiders, and New York Jets: Another four-time Super Bowl champion, Ronnie Lott was able to make his mark on the league by being a tough hitter, good perimeter defender, and excellent leader. While Joe Montana was the focal point of the team on offense, Lott was holding down the fort on defense. A Hall of Famer, many consider Lott to be the greatest safety of all time. I have a hard time disagreeing!

Cornerback:

Deion Sanders (1989–2000, 2004–2005) Played for the Atlanta Falcons, San Francisco 49ers, Dallas Cowboys, Washington Redskins, and Baltimore Ravens: Before Deion Sanders showed up, the cornerback position was not very glamorous. A lot of people made fun of the position and said it was for those people that couldn't make it as a receiver! Well, Deion "Primetime" Sanders helped change that notion. Fast, powerful, and elusive, Deion Sanders was able to shut down receivers while also being one of the greatest kick returners in NFL history. Once the ball was in his hands, he was nearly impossible to bring down with his combination of elusiveness and speed. In the modern-day NFL, cornerbacks are no longer disrespected like they were before Sanders took the field. He is a two-time Super Bowl champion and a Hall of Famer.

Basic Rules of NFL Football

Penalties

It's absurd how many things there are in football that are forbidden. Every time someone is found "committing an offence," they are subject to punishment, which typically entails a loss of yards. The ball is moved 10 yards away from the goal line if the offense receives a penalty of ten yards. The ball goes 10 yards closer to the goal line for every defensive penalty called. If the ball advances more than ten yards, or if the penalty clearly indicates that in addition to the amount of yards, it also includes an automatic first down, the number of downs does not change. The officials will announce that. Here are some of my favorite penalties:

- **Encroachment**. Before the ball is snapped, a defensive player crosses the line of scrimmage and makes contact with an opponent.

- **Offside**. At the time of the snap, a player from the offense or defense is on the incorrect side of the ball.

- **Delay of game**. Before the play clock runs out of time, the offense is unable to snap the ball.

- **Facemask**. You are not permitted to grasp a player by the facemask when tackling or blocking him. It is hazardous. A number of sanctions have been put in place to safeguard players against "extreme" harm.

- **Horse collar tackle**. Another extremely risky method of tackling a player is by grasping his shoulder pads and pushing him to the ground. When numerous players were hurt while being tackled in this way, it was declared unlawful.

- **Blocking below the waist**. Dangerous.

- **False start**. The offense cannot move once they have lined up until the ball has been snapped. A false start penalty can be incurred even with a slight head movement. By having the defender believe the ball is being snapped before it actually is, offenses attempt to deceive the defense. As they are immobile, they communicate "verbally."

- **Intentional grounding**. If there isn't a receiver available to catch the ball, the quarterback shouldn't throw it. When the quarterback senses that he is about to be sacked and is under pressure, it can be tempting to "throw the ball away." The ball is returned to the line of scrimmage by throwing a "incompletion". Furthermore, no yards were gained and none were lost. Without this rule, a quarterback would always "throw it away" while under pressure and unable to escape. As a result, there would never be a sack. However, if he is outside the "box," which is the space between the two offensive tackles on the line, he can still "throw it away." He is also permitted to discard it in a few other circumstances.

- **Holding**. This occurs when a player illegally restrains another player who is not in possession of the ball. This poses a risk and prevents players from enjoying the game as intended. This punishment is used frequently. Expect to see this one occur approximately every four plays. more frequently at times. Football can be challenging to play without "holding." When deciding what is holding and what isn't, the authorities have a lot of latitude.

- **Roughing**. It is forbidden to rough up the kicker, passer (quarterback), or snapper. This indicates that the player cannot be tackled after he has completed his task, such as passing, snapping, or kicking the ball, as doing so would only result in pain and harm. The rules have changed over time to better safeguard quarterbacks from harm. Following the release of the ball, a very light hit to the quarterback may result in a penalty.

- **Personal Foul**. This is typically used when a player simply punches someone for no reason. He is doing nothing to advance the game and only wants to cause suffering. A player might be out of bounds if they are lying on the ground. He gets jumped on by another player, who then elbows him. That would undoubtedly be reported. On the other hand, following a play, players occasionally become emotional and desire to continue the action with a fight. A call will go to that. Since the penalties are severe—15 yards and a first down if the offense is penalized—this is not a smart one to commit. This one generally gets players in trouble from their coaches because it is viewed as stupid. The players are expected to quit playing after the play is over.

- **Taunting**. It's one of my favorites! The wind may have been knocked out of a player at times, and they may be slow to get up after being on the ground. He's on the ground and a player from the other team is standing over him, saying things like, "That's right pal! More of that can be found in the same place! Then there's the ugly mother! similar matters. A mocking call may be issued for excessively celebrating. Teams may celebrate a little after a touchdown, but not excessively. The authorities may make these serious (15 yard) calls at their discretion.

- **Pass interference**. This might be a major challenge. The defensive player covering the receiver has few options if the quarterback throws to that receiver, making it difficult for him to interfere with the play. Certainly capable of intercepting passes, he can capture the ball. He is able to bat the ball away. There is no penalty if he makes contact with the receiver as he is pursuing the ball. However, pass interference occurs when a player makes contact with another player while not attempting to retrieve the ball, according to the referees.

In light of this, he is unable to tackle the player before he catches the ball.

If that were the case, all the defensive player would need to do to stop the receiver from ever getting the ball is to knock him down on each play. When pass interference is flagged, a first down is automatically awarded and the ball is spotted where the violation occurred. The ball is placed at the one-yard line and is an automatic first down if it occurs in the end zone. A pass completion is just as good as a pass interference call. It is now a first down at the location of the infraction, or the equivalent of a 50-yard pass completion, if the ball is thrown 50 yards but not completed because the receiver was impeded. This regulation has many nuances, so you have to see it in action a few times to have a sense of all the possible instances of pass interference.

Numerous other sanctions exist. Learn the ones I've listed before watching the game to pick up more.

Game Play

The game is played in four 15-minute increments, which rarely take exactly 15 minutes. The average game lasts somewhere between 2 and 3 hours, because the game clock stops between plays, and for other reasons such as:

- end of a quarter

- timeout

- 2-minute warning (the final 2 minutes of the 2nd & 4th quarters)

- penalty

- injury

- scoring

- possession change

- measuring a first down

Each team gets 4 tries, or downs, to move the ball toward the end zone. The offense loses possession of the ball by

- not moving the ball 10 yards in 4 downs

- scoring

- fumbling with recovery by the defense

- pass interception by the defense

- missing a field goal

- getting tackled in the end zone

Scoring

Touchdown – 6 points – when the offensive team crosses the goal line with the ball

Extra Point – 1 point – when the ball is kicked from the 15-yard line, between the uprights on the goal post following a touchdown

Field Goal – 3 points – can happen any time, but usually happens on the fourth down inside the 35-yard line. The ball is kicked between the uprights on the goal post

2-Point Conversion2 points – can take place instead of the extra point kick after a touchdown. The ball is placed on the 2-yard line, but instead of kicking it, the offensive team tries to move it past the goal line as in normal play. If the defense intercepts this ball, they can run it back to score 2 points

Safety2 Points – when the offense is tackled behind their goal line; can also happen if a dropped or blocked punt goes through the offensive end zone. Is sometimes awarded as a penalty, such as holding, in the end zone

Penalties

Only the most common; you may hear others during game play.

5 Yards

Delay of Game – the offense doesn't snap the ball before the 25 or 40 second play clock runs out

Offside – any part of a defensive player's body is across the line of scrimmage when the ball is snapped

False Start – anyone on the offensive line moves, except the man-in-motion, before the snap

Encroachment – a defensive player crosses the line of scrimmage and contacts an offensive player before the snap

Neutral Zone Infraction – a defensive player crosses the line of scrimmage before the snap and causes an offensive player to move

Illegal Formation – there must be 7 offensive players on the line of scrimmage, and every other player must be at least 1 yard behind them

Illegal Substitution – when more than 11 players break from the huddle. They must stay huddled until the extra player(s) are off the field

Illegal Motion – the players in the backfield move toward the line of scrimmage, instead of parallel to it, before the snap, or 2 players moving at the same time without resetting the ball

Illegal Contact – making contact with the receiver after the receiver has advanced more than 5 yards beyond the line of scrimmage, if the Quarterback is still in pocket and still has the ball

Holding (defense) – a defensive player holds or pulls an offensive player when more than 5 yards from the line of scrimmage

Too Many Players on the Field – there are more than 11 players on either side when the ball is snapped. An automatic first down is awarded to the offense when the defense is in violation

Ineligible Receiver Downfield (pass) – the ball is caught by any player other than a running back, wide receiver, or tight end

Ineligible Receiver Downfield (punt) – if anyone except the two players at the end of the line cross the line of scrimmage during a punt

10 Yards

Holding (offense) – an offensive player holds, grabs, or pulls a defensive player to keep him from progressing or gaining advantage

Pass Interference (offense) – when an offensive player keeps a defensive player from playing pass defense

Intentional Grounding – when the ball is thrown without a realistic chance of being caught

15 Yards

Personal Foul – a flagrant violation that causes injury to another player

Roughing the Passer – a defensive player makes contact with the Quarterback after he has passed the ball

Roughing the Kicker – a defensive player makes contact with the kicker before the kicker touches the ball

Face Mask – restraining a player by grabbing the facemask on the helmet

Unnecessary Roughness – using force beyond what is necessary to block or tackle another player

Unsportsmanlike Conduct (acting like a jackass on the field) – faking an injury, taunting, excessive celebration after a play, removing one's helmet on the field, leaving the bench to join a fight, etc.

The Most Important Schemes and Concepts in the NFL Today

When the NFL was founded in 1920, it was a very different league than the one we have today. Teams didn't have coaches, and they only had their own players to teach them the game and help them improve. There were no schemes or concepts; what you saw on the field was just 11 guys trying to outplay each other. As time went on, these 11 men began working together more effectively—and by doing so became a lot more entertaining to watch.

The Run-Pass Option

RPOs are a type of football play in which the quarterback has the option to either hand the ball off to the running back or pass it to a receiver or tight end. The idea is that this gives defenses multiple things to watch for and prevents them from teeing off on just one aspect of an offense's attack plan.

The concept has evolved over time, with many teams using RPOs differently than others depending on their personnel and scheme. For example, some teams will have a defensive end run-blitzing against an offensive tackle who's expecting help from his guard when he sees pressure from that side; other times you'll see offensive linemen blocking downfield on run plays only as decoys so that receivers can sneak behind them for big gains when defenders bite on their initial movement toward potential blocks.

The Pick Play

The pick play is a form of deception. The idea behind the concept is to get an offensive player open by having one teammate block for another, who then runs or passes the ball.

The pick play occurs when a receiver lines up on the line of scrimmage and performs what appears to be a blocking maneuver against an opposing defensive player. It's called a "pick" because that defender thinks he has first contact with someone other than the intended receiver, only for them both to separate at just enough time in order for him to be open for a pass or run (depending on what type of play was called). It's essentially legal cheating—a way around rules that prevent you from interfering with other players' routes because they're not technically being interfered with themselves; instead they're just playing along while their teammates take matters into their own hands and create openings where there were none before.

The Mesh Concept

The mesh concept is a passing concept that stretches the defense horizontally by forcing it to defend two routes at once. The receiver on the outside runs a vertical route, while the slot receiver runs an intermediate crossing pattern underneath it, creating what looks like a mesh between them. This allows both receivers to get open, while also stretching the defense in different areas so that they're not able to key in on where they need to be or who they need to cover.

The quarterback has options depending on how he reads this combination of routes and what kind of coverage he sees from the defense: He can throw either deep or short based on how he reads their coverage; if he thinks they're playing zone and want him to throw deep then he'll go for it; if he thinks they're man and want him throwing short then he'll do his best to find an open guy underneath first before trying any other plays because his receivers should have separation by now!

The Bunch Formation

The Bunch Formation is a formation where three or more receivers are lined up near the line of scrimmage. This is a pass-heavy formation that can create space for receivers, as well as confuse defenses.

In the bunch formation, multiple wide receivers will be "bunched" together on one side of the field. The offensive coordinator may choose to group them close together or spread them apart across the field in order to confuse defenses and create mismatches with slower linebackers and safeties who struggle to keep up with fast wideouts.

The Double Slant

The double slant is a very common concept in today's NFL, and it is used to stretch the defense horizontally. This allows the offense to create space for receivers and open up opportunities for big plays. The double slant also creates confusion for defenses because of its versatility. When executed correctly, this play can be very effective against man-to-man coverage or zone coverage as well as prevent defenses from overloading one side of the field with multiple defenders.

The Option Route

Option routes are a slightly more complex form of the slant and post routes.

The route is designed to get the receiver open in man-to-man coverage by taking advantage of defenders' tendency to overplay whichever route is run at that moment.

The idea behind an option route is that if a defender makes a mistake—either by creeping up too close to the line or retreating too far away from it—the receiver will have an open window through which he can work his way downfield. In other words, even though you're running one specific pattern (for example: a slant), you're actually looking for multiple ways out depending on how your defender reacts!

Option routes can be run by any receiver on a team's roster, regardless of size or speed; their success depends on understanding how defenses will react when they see different types of plays being called in advance."

Pre-Snap Motion

Pre-Snap Motion

Motion is the most important concept in today's NFL. It forces defenses to react and prepare for a variety of possible protections and routes, which often leads to confusion about where the ball will actually be thrown. In general terms, pre-snap movement involves players running to new positions before the snap of the ball. There are two main types: shifts and motions. Shifts involve moving one or more eligible receivers (i.e., those who line up outside of the tackle box) between multiple positions on one side of the formation while keeping other core players stationary; motion involves moving an ineligible receiver (i.e., those who line up inside of the tackle box) from one side to another after lining him up in an illegal position before doing so.*

Some teams use both types during a single play by having their quarterback run around first so that his receivers can get open later on in order for him not only throw them open but also confuse defensive backs into thinking they're making a mistake when they don't cover them as well as they could have if they had just stayed where they were supposed be during that play instead

The Bear Front

The bear front is a defensive alignment used by teams to defend the run, but it can also be used in pass coverage. The bear front is named after a formation used by the Chicago Bears in the 1940s and 1950s, so it's always been associated with Chicago football. Most people associate it with Bear Bryant's Alabama teams, which ran an extremely similar scheme under Bear Bryant's offense-based system from 1970 until his death in 1983.

The bear front uses three defensive linemen at the point of attack (two on either side of center), two linebackers who line up behind them (one outside each guard), and two safeties who are aligned behind each other near midfield (or just outside of it). What makes this defense unique is that each lineman has an assigned gap: one plays between center and guard; another plays between guard and tackle; another plays between tackle and tight end; while yet another plays just outside tight end to allow him to jam him off his route or pick him up if he gets past everyone else covering him.

The Roving Dime Defense

When a defense has only six defensive backs on the field, it's generally referred to as a "nickel." When you add another defensive back to this group, you get the "dime." This is how teams tend to play against three-receiver sets.

The Roving Dime Defense is important because it allows teams to have more flexibility in countering certain offensive concepts without sacrificing speed or coverage ability. The secondary is able to move around pre-snap and adjust their coverage based upon what they see from their opponent. So if your opponent goes into an empty set (no running back), then perhaps you'll move one of your safeties closer towards the line of scrimmage and turn them into linebackers so that they can cover any receivers who might get caught in traffic trying to get open downfield near the line of scrimmage. Or perhaps if your opponent motions a receiver from outside into tight slot position pre-snap, then maybe you'll move one of your corners over towards him instead so that he can match up with him when he comes out into route after motioning back across inside toward his own goal post after he gets out of motion (and maybe even before).

Pattern-Matching Coverage

Pattern-matching coverage is one of the most popular defensive schemes in football today. It's a zone coverage that allows defenses to match offensive formations and personnel.

Pattern-matching coverage has grown in popularity over the last 15 years because it allows defenses to defend against multiple types of pass plays at once: quick passes, intermediate passes, and deep balls. In addition, pattern matching helps defend against bunch formations (where three or more receivers line up on one side) by disrupting the timing and order of routes run by receivers from different areas on the field.

The defense can also use pattern-matching technique to disguise blitzes or blitz packages by flipping its assignments based on whether an offense has sent out two backs or only one back into pass protection. Pattern matching also enables defenses to play man coverage in certain situations; for example, when a slot receiver aligns inside another receiver but isn't part of his progression route tree—a concept we'll discuss later—the defense can cover him with a linebacker instead of a cornerback because he won't get open anyway if he doesn't get separation from his defender due to poor position/technique during his release off the line scrimmage

This sport is growing in complexity with each passing year.

The NFL is a complicated sport, and it's only getting more complicated. Even if you know that the league has been around since 1920, that doesn't mean you understand every aspect of its modern incarnation. In fact, a lot of people who follow football closely—and even some who don't—can be confused by all the different schemes and concepts that are thrown around during broadcasts and in articles about football strategy.

The good news is that you don't have to be an expert to watch or read about football these days. You just need some basic knowledge about what's going on out there on the field so that when someone says something like "the offense shifts from 11 personnel into 22 personnel against this defense" or "he was lined up in an inverted V," for example, you'll know what they're talking about without having to look up those terms online later.

While the NFL is certainly a complex game, it has shown that it can be mastered by anyone with the right tools. In this article, we've provided you with some of the most important concepts and schemes in the league today so that you can better understand what makes professional football so entertaining to watch.

Chapter 5

FOOTBALL AT COLLEGE

If you are interested in playing college football, you have come to the right place! This guide will give you all the information that you need to know to become a successful player with your college team.

American football is a physically demanding sport that requires players to be in top physical condition. To play football, you need to be able to run and jump at high speeds, tackle an opponent with force, and make quick decisions on the field. Football is also a full-contact sport that can cause injuries such as broken bones or concussions. Players must learn to protect themselves while still aggressively playing against opponents.

To prepare for college football season, you should start strength exercises using weights or resistance bands at least three months before your first practice begins. This will help build muscle mass so you're fast enough to compete on the field without getting too tired during games or practices.

You should also do cardiovascular activities such as jogging every day during this time period so that your heart rate increases gradually over time rather than suddenly when practicing starts

The first step to becoming a football player is getting into shape. You don't have to be 6'3" and 240 pounds, but you do need to be able to run fast and jump high. You'll also need the strength to lift weights and perform other exercises.

And, of course, there's no way you can play if you're afraid of being hit or hurt!

The second step is learning how to pass or catch a ball: throw it straight ahead; throw it overhand; kick the ball with your foot; bounce it off your knee into a teammate's hands—there are lots of ways for players on both sides of the ball (the offense versus defense) to score points in their favor by scoring touchdowns whenever possible during each game day.

Football is a team sport, so you need to be able to work together as a team. Teamwork is important in football. You need to work together as a team and communicate with your teammates. You also have to be able to trust your teammates and know that they will support you when you're in trouble.

It's not enough to just love football. You need to focus on your training and conditioning if you want to compete at the highest levels of the game. Football players have a lot of things going on in their lives, but if you want to reach college level and beyond you need to be ready for it.

Here are some tips for improving your game:

• Train hard during the off season so that when preseason hits, your body is ready for the demands of practice and games.

• Eat healthy foods with lots of protein—chicken, fish and lean beef are good examples. Protein helps build muscle which will help you run faster when it matters most during games!

You need good hand-eye coordination and balance to excel at American football.

Hand-eye coordination is an important skill for all the players on the field, but it's especially important for quarterbacks, wide receivers and defensive backs. These athletes must be able to catch passes thrown by other players and intercept balls that are thrown their way. They also have to be able to block or tackle opposing players who are trying to make plays on them.

Offensive linemen have to have excellent hand-eye coordination too—they need to be able to block defensive linemen from tackling their quarterback or running back, as well as tackle opposing linebackers when they're trying to stop those same offensive players from scoring touchdowns or advancing downfield toward scoring positions like first downs.

The most important characteristic in a quarterback is confidence in his abilities, which comes from working hard. If you're going to be a successful college football player, you need to work hard at everything you do on the field and off of it. The best players understand that they have to work as hard as possible if they want to succeed at their sport.

For example, Andrew Luck worked very hard during his time at Stanford University so that he could become one of the best quarterbacks in college football history and get drafted by the Indianapolis Colts as number one overall pick in 2012. By working harder than everyone else and being willing to put in extra effort during practice sessions, Luck was able to become a great player despite not being blessed with exceptional athleticism or size compared with other quarterbacks like Robert Griffin III who were also playing college football around this same time period (Griffin played for Baylor University).

In general terms: if I could give advice about anything related with sports then it would be about how important it is for kids especially young ones between ages 14-18 years old because these are usually considered formative years where people develop good habits or bad ones depending on how much effort they put into things such as studying hard enough so that their grades don't suffer when school starts back up again after summer break ends."

In order to play quarterback in college football, you need to have a strong arm and quick release. This is because the offense can only work if the ball is delivered accurately and quickly. Imagine if your quarterback had a weak arm: it would take forever for him to get rid of the ball, which would make it easy for defenders to catch up with him. If he couldn't throw fast enough, then he'd be sacked constantly by defensive linemen who could easily get past their blockers.

For example, think about Drew Brees and Tom Brady—they both have great arms that allow them to zip passes all over the field at high speeds without having to worry about being tackled behind the line of scrimmage before they're done throwing. They've also been able to stay healthy during their careers due in part because they don't take too many hits from opposing players who might otherwise knock them out of games permanently!

There are also some other types of quarterbacks who don't necessarily have strong arms but still manage well enough on offense because they know how much pressure should go into each pass (this depends partly on distance). These QBs usually do better when paired with teams that run short routes like slants or sideline outs instead because these passes give less room for error compared with deep balls where everything needs perfect timing before completion will likely occur successfully."

If you play football for your college, it will be easy for you to get into law school or medical school after graduation because of the many connections you've made through playing with other players from colleges around the country! If you're interested in studying law, getting a degree in philosophy or English can help. With these skills, you can work as an editor at a publishing company. You could also become an attorney if that's something that interests you.

If medicine is more up your alley but your science grades aren't up to par, try taking classes at community colleges while still attending your main college; this way, you'll have time to improve before entering medical school.

One of the best ways for an aspiring college student athlete wanting to play Division I football is by participating in youth leagues such as Pop Warner football. This is a great way to get noticed by college coaches, as well as get in shape and learn the fundamentals of the game. It's also a great way to make friends, which will help prepare you for being on campus once you've graduated high school.

If you're interested in playing football at a high level, then it's important to start working at it early. The best way to do this is by participating in youth leagues such as Pop Warner or similar organizations that are focused on developing young players into future college athletes.

Chapter 6

GIRLS FOOTBALL

In recent years, there has been a growing awareness of the role of women in football, and women are now able to compete on an equal footing with men. But despite this progress, there is still a lot of work to do if we are going to allow women to have the same opportunities as men in this sport. Women should be allowed to play football just as much as men do; it's time for them to get their chance!

There's no denying that women footballers have to work a lot harder to be taken seriously. They are not considered professional, and they don't get paid as much as men. They also don't get the same opportunities as their male counterparts—for example, only one league in Europe plays with a full-size pitch (the men's Premier League).

The game is growing rapidly worldwide, with over 300 million players and counting. But if we're going to make women's football as popular as its male counterpart, we need more than just hard work—we need commitment from those who hold power at clubs and federations.

If you are thinking about playing football, then take the time to read this article and find out how you can get started. There are many people who have done it before, so there is no reason why you can't do it too!

Women in football face a lot of opposition and sexism. They are not given the same opportunities as men, they're paid less, they're taken less seriously, and on top of all this, they have to work twice as hard just to be taken as an equal.

Consider these statistics: women make up only 7% of referees at professional level in England's Premier League; 77% of sports editors in newspapers are male; only 3% of sports editors in TV stations are female; the majority (62%) of the workforce within sports media is white - compared with 48% across all industries; only 25% in radio broadcasting are BAME (black Asian minority ethnic) compared with 49% across all industries."

While people were slow to realise it, women's football has been around for a very long time. Indeed, the Women's Football Association (WFA) was founded in 1969 and the first official women's football match took place in 1895 - a full 15 years before the Football Association (FA).

The FA was established in 1863 and its founding members included famous figures like Ebenezer Cobb Morley and other gentlemen who believed that football should be "an open field for all". This shows just how little has changed over time; while women were denied access to playing on some pitches because they weren't considered fit enough, they have now proven themselves capable of competing on equal terms with men. And yet many people still believe that female athletes aren't as good at their sport as male ones!

Football has always been a male-dominated sport. Women have not been considered strong enough to play football, and society has been slow to change this view. Women were not allowed to play football until the 1970s, when the first professional team was created in Britain.

As you may know, football is a sport that was originally only for men. This is because it used to be seen as a dangerous sport for women, who were supposed to stay home and be housewives. Women weren't allowed to play football or other sports until the 19th century and even then they weren't allowed to be athletes. The first women's football team was founded in Scotland in 1881 but they had to wear men's clothes so nobody would know they were female!

Football is the most popular sport in the world, with over 250 million people playing the game every week. It's also one of the few sports that has a huge following among women, who make up some 20% of football fans globally.

Nowadays more and more girls are playing football in school and for clubs; they're getting more opportunities to play professionally too. In fact, there are now around 100 professional female players across Europe's top leagues like England's WSL1 or Germany's Bundesliga Frauen–and this number is growing every year!

There are many great female players out there who play for clubs in the UK and even internationally.

- Katrine Veje

- Ada Hegerberg

- Kim Little

- Amelia Ritchie

Women can succeed in football if given the same opportunities as men.

Despite the progress of women's football, there is still a long way to go before we can say that it is truly on par with men's football. The biggest issue facing women in football right now is that they are not considered professional players by FIFA or UEFA. Women's teams are not given equal playing time or prize money as their male counterparts, meaning that women have less opportunities for exposure and growth.

If you were asked to name 10 famous female footballers, what would you say? Now ask yourself how many male players you could name from memory— the chances are pretty slim for both lists being identical! While this imbalance may be as a result of sexism within the sport itself, another factor could also be at play: lack of exposure and support from sponsors who might otherwise invest in female teams if they were seen to have potential profit potential like their male counterparts do (think about how Nike sponsors Ronaldo but not any female footballers).

If you are interested in playing football, there is no better time than now. There are so many great female players out there who have achieved success and proven that women can succeed in football just as well as men. It's not just about having fun on the pitch or making friends with other girls; it's also about being able to show off your skills and proving that women can be just as good at this game as men!

FINAL WORDS

From its origins in rugby, American football has evolved into the most popular spectator sport in America. At the core of the game is a set of tactics and techniques for carrying out specific tasks on the field. The most familiar of these is the "passing" technique that uses an elongated ball to throw from one player to another. In recent years, women have joined men as players in this challenging endeavor and also as fans who enjoy watching it on television.

Part of what makes football so attractive is not simply the strategy required to succeed in it, but more importantly, the passion fans invest in their teams. The teams vie for prize money and public recognition through wins and championships. Yet in many ways, football remains a sport that hinges on its age-old strategy of getting the ball into scoring position within a designated area of the field governed by lines called "goal" lines.

With the game becoming more and more popular, there has been a trend towards more advanced plays. Rules have changed to allow for two-point conversions after touchdowns and much harsher penalties have started to be imposed on players who break the rules of playing hard. But even with all of these changes, fans will find much to love about the game in this book.

I hope you enjoy it!

Made in the USA
Middletown, DE
19 January 2023

22571743R00057